SPOTLIGHT ON CHILDREN'S AUTHORS

# WALTER DEAN MYERS

RICHARD ANDERSEN

Cavendish Square
New York

*For Mon Petite Chou Polonaise*

Published in 2014 by Cavendish Square Publishing, LLC
303 Park Avenue South, Suite 1247, New York, NY 10010
Copyright © 2014 by Cavendish Square Publishing, LLC
First Edition

Library of Congress Cataloging-in-Publication Data
Andersen, Richard, 1946–
Walter Dean Myers / Richard Andersen.
pages cm. — (Spotlight on children's authors)
Includes bibliographical references and index.
ISBN 978-1-62712-262-7 (hardcover) ISBN 978-1-62712-263-4 (paperback) ISBN 978-1-62712-264-1 (ebook)
1. Myers, Walter Dean, 1937– Juvenile literature. 2. Authors, American—20th century—Biography—Juvenile literature.
3. African American authors—Biography—Juvenile literature. 4. Children's stories—Authorship—Juvenile literature. I.
Title.
PS3563.Y48Z55 2014
813'.54—dc23
2013030147

Editorial Director: Dean Miller
Senior Editor: Peter Mavrikis
Copy Editor: Cynthia Roby
Art Director: Jeffrey Talbot
Designer: Amy Greenan
Production Manager: Jennifer Ryder-Talbot
Production Editor: Andrew Coddington
Photo research by Julie Alissi, J8 Media

The photographs in this book are used by permission and through the courtesy of: Cover photo by AP Photo/Charles Sykes; Museum of the City of New York/Contributor/Archive Photos/Getty Images, 4; Robert W. Kelley/Contributor/Time & Life Pictures/Getty Images, 5; AP Photo/Mark Godfrey, 6; © Scholastic, 7 ; Perry H Kretz/Hulton Archive/Getty Images, 8; AP Photo/Charles Sykes, 10; Adrian Assalve/E+/Getty Images, 11; © Random House, 12; Sam Edwards/Caiaimage/Getty Images, 17; Tim Santimore/Photolibrary/Getty Images, 18; Dennis Brack/Newscom, 21; AP Photo/Charles Sykes, 22; NICHOLAS KAMM/Staff/AFP/Getty Images, 25; © Harper Collins, 26; HUGH GRANNUM/KRT/Newscom, 28; © David R. Frazier Photolibrary, Inc/Alamy, 30; Flirt / SuperStock, 33; © Nancy Kaszerman/ZUMA Press, 34; © Harper Collins, 36; © AP Images, 37; AP Photo/Charles Sykes, 38; © Penguin, 39.

Printed in the United States of America

# CONTENTS

## INTRODUCTION: "Whatever Happens, Don't Stop Writing."

WALTER DEAN MYERS let his fists do the talking. By the time he was in the fourth grade, he'd beaten up so many kids and spent so much time in the principal's office he was about to be expelled. Fortunately, an attack of appendicitis kept him out of school until it was closed for the summer. What had Walter's classmates done to deserve such poundings? They teased him when he couldn't pronounce certain words the same way they did. He never knew that he had a speech impediment because his mom and dad and two sisters always understood what he had to say.

Walter did other things besides clobber people. He held hands with some of the children who lived on his street, and sang religious hymns with them as they walked to and from Sunday school. He learned to love reading from the *True Romance Magazine* stories his mom shared with him at their kitchen table in Harlem. He developed ways of creating suspense from listening to the stories his father told when he came home from work.

In Walter's day—he was born in 1937—the streets and parks of Harlem were safe. The music of Duke Ellington and Count Basie poured from the buildings, and it wasn't unusual for Walter to see heroes like the boxers Joe Louis and Sugar Ray Robinson strolling down 125th Street. The poet Langston Hughes was there too.

Harlem also had its share of crime and violence. A young boy could easily be distracted from the values he was taught at home, school, and church. Walter had his share of wayward distractions, but he also had sports (he was a talented basketball player); books (they helped pass time in the principal's office); and writing (a practice he developed when his fourth grade teacher—whom he'd hit with a book—suggested he write what he had trouble saying).

Famous poet, playwright, and essayist, Langston Hughes stands on the stoop of his apartment building in Harlem.

Then in high school a seed was planted. Walter was sitting outside the guidance counselor's office while his mother was inside learning that her son had missed thirty days of school. His English teacher walked by. "Whatever happens, don't stop writing," Mrs. Liebow told him. Walter couldn't imagine making his living as a writer, but his reason for writing changed. Writing became

More than 52,000 American soldiers and 2 million Vietnamese lost their lives in a war that Walter refers to as "an obscene waste."

an opportunity to explore the part of him that few people knew. It was the part that the fighter and the athlete kept hidden because it wasn't considered "manly" by those in his community. Along with the books that Walter carried in his hand, there was also a stiletto in his pocket.

By the time he was sixteen, it became clear to Walter that he couldn't continue to live as he had been. He dropped out of school, and was even in danger of being arrested. As he saw it, he had four choices: shape up, ship out, go to prison, or die. Walter chose to ship out. He celebrated his seventeenth birthday by enlisting in the United States Army.

Walter spent three awful years in the military, although the only serious shots he fired were at basketball hoops. Several low-paying jobs, including construction worker, followed his discharge. Walter had just about given up on writing. One day, he remembered what his English teacher had told him: "Whatever happens, don't stop writing." That day, covered with the dirt and debris that came from knocking down walls with a sledgehammer, he bought a composition book.

Once Walter started writing again, he couldn't stop. There were more rejections of his work than acceptances, but it didn't matter. He realized after reading James Baldwin's story "Sonny Blues" how powerful his writing could become if he wrote about his own experiences in his own voice. He wrote about the subjects he knew best: basketball, the army, and Harlem. Basketball became the vehicle for one of the best sports novels ever written: *Hoops*. Walter's first army story was published by *Essence* magazine. The death of his twenty-one-year-old younger brother in Vietnam served as an inspiration for him to write his masterpiece: *Fallen Angels*. You can think of *Monster* as the story of what might have happened to Walter had he not had the loving mom who taught him to read, the caring dad who bought him his first typewriter, and the insightful teacher who told him to keep writing no matter what happens.

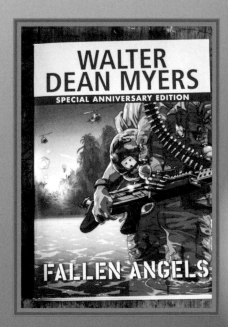

Cover of *Fallen Angels*. Walter reminds us how young most soldiers are and how difficult it is to grow up under the conditions brought about by war.

Metal or wooden backboards, chain-link nets, and unforgiving rims force New York City playground players to sharpen their shooting skills from a very young age.

# Chapter 1
# HOOPS (1981)

Meet Lonnie Jackson. Well, Lonnie is the boy **Walter** could have been had he made better choices in his teenage years. Like Lonnie, Walter was a tremendously talented basketball player. Growing up, he got to play with boys four and five years older. That's a sign of a good player in any community, but in Harlem, it was nothing less than superb. But like a lot of immature kids with more talent than they know what to do with, Walter was attracted to what he calls "the mystique of the semi-hoodlum." Walter dropped out of high school at sixteen to hang full-time with drug dealers in Morningside Park. Then he dropped out a second time because he heard the police were looking for him. If he didn't get out of town, there was a good chance he would be arrested. That's when he enlisted in the army.

Walter played a lot of ball in the army, but not enough to truly advance his game. He continued playing after he was discharged in 1957, and by 1961 he was playing for a team called the Jolly Brown Giants. Walter's last serious shot at a basket was taken in 1966 at the Cage, a famous outdoor court boxed in by a tall chain-

Walter says he didn't play well with others as a child, so he learned to create his own characters through writing: "I play quite well with them."

link fence in New York's Greenwich Village. Players with names like Helicopter wouldn't pick him for their team because they didn't think he could help them win. Walter wasn't doing so well off the court either. Married with two kids, he spent most of his time with artists in the East Village, played percussion instruments in a band, and dreamed of what might have been. *Hoops* is that dream.

Like Walter at seventeen, Lonnie Jackson's got game. He's also got issues. He can't tell his girlfriend he loves her because she's shown how much he means to her. Walter didn't have a girlfriend at this age—he was more into sports and writing—but if he could have had one, she would have been like Mary-Ann. She adores Lonnie, and Lonnie doesn't have to do much to merit her affection.

Then there's Coach Cal, the father Walter wishes he had. Walter's biological father allowed his former wife and her second husband to informally adopt the two-year-old boy in 1940 after his biological mother died giving birth to what would have been a younger sister. Walter's adoptive father loved the boy as if he were his own son, but he never praised him for anything he wrote. Nevertheless, Mr. Dean was the one who bought Walter his first typewriter when he was fifteen years old, a gift for which Walter shows his appreciation in his dedication of *Hoops*: "To My Father, Herbert Dean, who bought my first typewriter for me."

When Walter's father gave him a typewriter for his fifteenth birthday, he never imagined his son would someday be a famous writer.

walter dean myers

HOOPS

For many kids growing up in Harlem, basketball is seen as a ticket out of the ghetto and on to success. Drugs are often seen the same way.

Mr. Dean must have seen the typewriter as a toy or a part of phase his son was going through because he worried that Walter was still writing long after he'd been discharged from the army. In Mr. Dean's mind, writing wasn't a reliable way for a "man" to earn a living. Even after Walter was able to support himself and his family on the money he made from his writing, Mr. Dean had nothing good to say about anything he wrote. It wasn't until after Mr. Dean died in 1986 that Walter discovered his father couldn't read, and that he'd been too embarrassed to let either the boy, or the author he became, know.

This is where Coach Cal comes in. Like the father that Walter wishes he had, he wants Lonnie to bring himself and his game to higher levels, but Lonnie thinks he's already got all it takes to score—on and off the court. Cal's got issues too. A point shaver as a college student, he's now under pressure by some heavy bettors to keep Lonnie on the bench so his team will come up short in its championship game.

Mary-Ann is Lonnie's girlfriend though he hasn't done anything to make it official. That's because he knows he doesn't have to. Mary-Ann is crazy about him. She also has a brother Paul, who's been flashing a lot of money lately to try to impress a woman. Paul used to be Lonnie's main main, but they haven't seen much of each other lately because Paul is secretly stealing welfare checks, which he sells to Mary-Ann's boss Tyrone at an after-hours bar. Paul performs other felony services as well. One of the more seemingly innocent ones is to help organize a basketball tournament in which Lonnie has been chosen to play. It's a big deal. Scouts are going to show up at a televised championship game in Madison Square Garden. This is going to be Lonnie's first step out of Harlem and into the limelight. It's all part of his game plan.

Cal Jones isn't. When we first meet him, he's lying spread-eagle and drunk in the middle of a playground basketball court. When Lonnie discovers that this rundown relic is going to coach the tournament team, "cool" is not the first word to enter his head. The next time the two meet, it's on a court. Cal challenges Lonnie to a game of one-on-one and beats him easily—a lesson in "manhood" that's not lost on the boy. More respect for the coach comes when Lonnie discovers that Cal is the same Cal Jones who was one of the student athletes involved in the point-shaving scandal that rocked City College during the mid-1950s and which Walter, living in Harlem, would have been well aware of. That Cal engaged in an illegal activity doesn't bother Lonnie. He's used to all sorts of crime. The past bothers Cal, however. Barred from participating on a professional level, the coaching gig is his chance at redemption. So is Lonnie, but Lonnie doesn't know that yet. Neither does Cal. How their relationship develops and what becomes of it is what *Hoops* is really all about.

As Cal raises the playing level of Lonnie's basketball skills, Lonnie learns from him how easy it is for people to give in to the temptation of quick and easy money and what can happen when the gains are illegal. He's not only lost out on a career in basketball, he's lost out on his marriage. Now Cal wants to show Lonnie that there are more important things in life than basketball, and that he needs to develop a sense of integrity to go along with his skills on the court.

The more Lonnie learns about Cal, the more he likes him. But he's never quite sure how far the coach can be trusted when he misses two of the early games in the tournament. What's that about? And how much of it has to do with Mary-Ann's boss, Tyrone? As you might expect, a lot. Tyrone's got money and his rep as a fixer riding on the scoreboard, and all he has to do to succeed is have Cal keep Lonnie warming pine until the game is out of reach.

Cal, of course, has other plans, but he needs Lonnie to trust him. This is no easy task. Especially after Lonnie learns that his coach has bet $2,000 on the opposing team. He's also let it be known that his star can't play because of a bad ankle. Nevertheless, Lonnie agrees to begin the game on his bottom and keep his eyes on Tyrone and his posse in the stands.

Lonnie's teammates keep the score close, but when it seems the time clock has turned irretrievably against them, Tyrone places his final bets. That's when Cal places his redemption in Lonnie's hands: "You can go out there and do nothing and throw away the game. Or you can go out there and play like you know you can and we can take this whole thing. We can bust Tyrone's action. I can't do it, man, but you can."

The young man beautifully feeds the ball to another player for the winning basket in the final seconds. But then there's the matter of Tyrone, who quickly ushers Cal into the locker room. By the time Lonnie gets there, Cal has been turned into a punching bag. Lonnie grabs the homeboy that's holding him, and Cal goes after Tyrone, but the gangster carries a knife and knows how to use it. Cal goes down, the bad guys escape, and Lonnie is left to hold his beloved coach until he breathes his last breath.

And you thought *Hoops* is about basketball. A lot of it is, but like all serious works of literature, *Hoops* transcends its geographical location (Harlem) and subject category (sports) to touch the minds and hearts of readers of all ages and backgrounds. Readers who see themselves reflected in the lives of Lonnie, Cal, and other characters even when those lives seem so different from their own. For Walter Dean Myers, the central themes of this book are love, friendship, trust, loyalty, perseverance, courage, and redemption, and the role they play in the life of a boy about to cross the threshold of adult responsibility. That Walter presents them through basketball is only one measurement of his literary genius.

Unlike hardwood floors, asphalt doesn't just burn when you fall on it; it cuts into you. Growing up poor and feeling alone in the world can cut into you in other, deeper ways.

More people died of war-related causes in the twentieth century than all the people who died in all the previous wars in history put together.

# Chapter 2
# FALLEN ANGELS (1988)

Walter Dean Myers dedicated *Fallen Angels* to his younger brother Sonny, who died on his first combat patrol in Vietnam on May 7, 1968. He was only twenty-one years old and had enlisted in the army, in part, to gain the respect and admiration he saw given to Walter by members of his family when he was in uniform from 1954 to 1957. In an attempt to lessen the guilt he carried for any role he might have played in his brother's senseless death, Walter wrote his most highly acclaimed work: *Fallen Angels*.

Like *Hoops*, *Fallen Angels* is a coming-of-age story. In *Fallen Angels*, Richie Perry grows from an innocent young man to an adult who learns more about the world than he will ever want to know. Richie, like Lonnie, is based on Walter's own life. Both Richie and Walter are from Harlem. They both drop out of Stuyvesant High School where they were taught by Mrs. Bonnie Liebow— the woman who told Walter to keep on writing—and enlist in the army and play basketball. They both have impressionable younger brothers who look up to them. The major difference between Richie and Walter is that Walter never experienced combat.

To narrate the hurry-up-and-wait drudgery of everyday military life, Walter relied on his own army experience. Describing a firefight was a different story. To prepare for these parts of his narrative, Walter researched all the major events of the Vietnam War using the National Archives in Washington, DC. He interviewed people from the Vietnam Veterans Outreach Center and traveled across the country to get to know the places where the book's characters lived before they enlisted.

When we first meet Richie Perry, he is nothing like the gung ho type of soldier you usually see in movies and on television. During a touchdown in Alaska, you meet Pewee Gates, an irreverent recruit whose sense of humor provides Richie with temporary relief from the long hours of boredom and moments of sheer terror that await them. "Where the hell is your pride, soldier?" a captain asks Peewee. "In Chicago, sir. Can I go get it?"

To combat the hours of waiting for what they believe will be a marvelous adventure, the men play checkers, chess, cards, and Ping-Pong. They write letters, drink beer, and get into fights with one another. They listen to the radio, keep their rifles clean, and dream of home.

For the moments of terror, there is no relief. They linger in the minds of the soldiers long after the events have passed. Richie and Peewee watch their comrade Jenkins die from a booby trap in a rice paddy on his very first combat patrol—much like Walter's brother Sonny. Only a few hundred yards from their camp, the soldiers thought they were safe. They soon learn they never are. It

These metal tags are worn around the neck and used to identify the bodies of dead soldiers even when the tags are all that's left of them.

gets worse, and Richie stares death in the face as he looks down the barrel of an AK-47.

Providing a bizarre kind of background music for all of the above are the sounds of whirling helicopters, strafing machine guns, and terrifying firefights. They're as constant as the mosquitoes, rodents,

"I tried to figure out who I was in a world that often seemed hostile. I'm still resolving these issues." —Walter Dean Myers

# A DAY IN THE LIFE OF
# WALTER DEAN MYERS:

Wake up at 4:30 a.m. Lie in bed thinking about what to write.

Get up at 5:00 a.m. for a morning walk.

Review outlines by 7:00 a.m., start writing, and enjoy every minute of it.

Aim toward goal of five pages. Once achieved, head for the post office.

Review five pages, revise outline, and think about the next day's work.

Practice playing flute or reading in the afternoon.

Answer correspondences.

Go for another walk.

Prepare dinner (Walter shares the cooking with his wife, Joyce).

Sit down with a crossword puzzle.

Be in bed by 10:00 p.m.

and leeches, the mass burnings of bodies, the collection of dog tags, the counting of body bags, and the killing of people to put them out of their misery.

*Fallen Angels* provides examples of the surreal nature of military life. Imagine destroying one village along with almost everyone in it and then trying to endear yourself to the residents of another with handouts of bandages, malaria pills, and chocolate bars. Imagine providing protection for a civilian pacification team showing Donald Duck cartoons while behind the movie screen a fighter jet goes down with its pilots following shortly afterwards in parachutes. Imagine unnecessarily risking the lives of the soldiers under your command and inflating the body counts of dead Vietcong to win a promotion.

Richie tries to write to his mom to ensure her that he is okay. He also wants to prevent his little brother from making the same mistake he has by telling him what war is really like. But he can't find the words to do either. Only four months "in country" and he's already been wounded in several places. The Purple Heart medal he receives means nothing to him. Nor do the words of army chaplain Father Santora: "Prayer can be very comforting."

What is comforting to Richie? The presence and support of Peewee Gates. After swearing a vow of friendship, Peewee stays with Richie until a bad case of diarrhea passes and holds him until he stops shaking from the trauma of having been nearly killed. Peewee also makes Richie realize that they're not in Vietnam to prevent the spread of communism. Nor are they necessarily the good guys. Their number one priority is to survive. That means to either kill or be killed.

For the author, who became a pacifist after his brother died in Vietnam, war is more than a question of survival. There are lessons you can learn from being in combat—the importance of friendship, trust, and loyalty—but you don't have to either kill or risk being killed to learn them. War, as it is represented in *Fallen Angels*, is nothing more than an obscene waste.

Among the names of dead soldiers listed on the walls of the Vietnam Memorial is that of Walter's younger brother: Thomas Wayne "Sonny" Myers. He was only twenty-one years old.

WALTER DEAN MYERS

MONSTER

NATIONAL BOOK AWARD
FINALIST

--17 -12 /59-4 8-2

STATE

In Monster, Walter
wants us to ask
ourselves, "Is it possible
to be legally innocent
and morally guilty at
the same time?"

# Chapter 3

# MONSTER
## (1999)

Walter Dean Myers laid the groundwork for *Monster* fifteen years before he sat down to write it. In one of several attempts to convince his father he was a serious writer, he took courses in criminal justice while working on his bachelor's degree in communications at Empire State College in New York. For a project that grew to more than 600 pages, Walter interviewed scores of lawyers, murderers, thieves, prostitutes, drug dealers, and juvenile delinquents who'd been incarcerated for crimes they'd committed in part because there was no adult in their lives who could adequately supervise them. He learned a great deal about how the criminal justice system worked, but what impressed Walter most was how the inmates talked about their cases. They never addressed the issue of moral responsibility. It was almost as if they'd committed a criminal action but were innocent of having done anything wrong.

A spike in the rate of violent crimes committed by teenagers in 1997 motivated Walter to revisit the project he'd completed in 1983. He attended a criminal justice seminar presented by the New York City's prosecutor's office, and then sat in on the trial of a seventeen-year-old boy charged with armed robbery and attempted murder. Walter realized that, had he not enlisted in the army at the same age as the boy on trial, he might have wound up facing similar charges. Walter hoped that by writing *Monster* he'd put a human face on the kids who were being represented as monsters in the news media. The story of Steve Harmon, the protagonist of *Monster*, could easily have been the story of Walter Dean Myers had he not enlisted in the army in 1954. In some ways, the book serves as a confession for crimes Walter committed, but for which he was never held accountable.

The first thing you notice about *Monster* is that it isn't like any novel you've ever seen. The early pages are taken from a handwritten journal. Then what's obviously a screenplay appears. But the handwritten pages don't go away. Every so often they interrupt and comment on what's taking place in the screenplay. Punctuating the screenplay and the comments are some photos of a kid in a striped shirt. There's even a courtroom drawing like the kind you see on television, and the fingerprints on the jacket cover belong to Walter Dean Myers. What's this all about?

The kid in the photo is sixteen-year-old Steve Harmon. He's on trial for aiding and abetting an attempted robbery that turned into a murder. Inspired by his filmmaking teacher at Stuyvesant High School, Steve has decided to make a movie of the proceedings. Only courtroom dramas don't show the thoughts that can go through a defendant's head. Their focus is on the action before the bench. So whenever Steve feels the need to comment, he writes what he wants to say in his journal. This is his way of contradicting how he is

## WALTER DEAN MYERS' ADVICE TO YOUNG WRITERS:

"The most important skill is the ability to use language. You learn language from other people—from reading people who are good. So you have to be a good reader. The second most important skill is discipline. You sit down and you start something, and you have to finish it."

Most readers are relieved when
Steve Harmon is found not
guilty, but Walter wants us to be
bothered by the possible role he
played in an innocent man's murder.

sometimes portrayed in the courtroom. The prosecuting attorney, for example, refers to him early on as a "monster." Steve's attorney finds the image troubling. Because Steve is young, the adults in the jury may think of him as less responsible. Because he's African American, their internalized racism may lead them to assume he is more likely to be guilty than a white defendant. And why else would Steve be on trial if he hadn't done something wrong? It wouldn't take a great leap of the imagination for the jury to picture the young, African-American defendant as a monster before his trial even began. "You better put some distance between yourself and whatever you think a tough guy represents," Steve's attorney tells him. To which Steve replies in his journal: "I want to look like a good person. I want to feel like a good person because I believe I am."

In addition to commenting on the drama taking place in the courtroom, Steve includes in his journal observations of what it is like to be in prison, starting with the opening line of the novel: "The best time to cry is at night, when the lights are out and someone is being beaten up and screaming for help." When the prisoners are not beating up on one and other, they talk about what got them locked up, but it's clear to Steve that they're lying to each other, and after they've lied so much for so long, they've come to believe their stories are true, which makes Steve wonder how much of what he tells himself is lies. When he looks in a mirror, he hardly recognizes himself. Is that because life in prison is dehumanizing or is the image Walter Myers' metaphor for what's taking place in Steve's conscience? How about both?

In contrast with what takes place inside the cells is the action that occurs in the visiting room when Steve's parents come to be with their son. Steve's mother is a religious woman who gives Steve a Bible with marked passages from the Book of Psalms. No matter what the jury decides, she knows he is innocent. Steve's father, unlike the fathers in *Hoops* and *Fallen Angels*, is not an absentee parent. A college-educated professional, he can't believe a son of his could wind up in a place like the one described in the novel. When he breaks down, it is the first time Steve has ever seen him cry. After the jury reaches its decision to acquit, the father says he is thankful Steve does not have to go to jail, but an emotional distance has surfaced between them. Steve comments, "My father is no longer sure of who I am." Neither is Steve at this point. How did he go from being a student at one of the best public high schools in New York City to associating with petty criminals such as Bobo and King to a frightened boy in a prison cell in just a few months? "That's why I want to take the films of myself," Steve writes in his journal. "I want to know who I am."

Like *Hoops* and *Fallen Angels*, Monster is a coming-of-age story. But unlike Lonnie Jackson and Richie Perry, Steve Harmon doesn't cross the threshold of adulthood by accepting responsibility for any part he may have played in the robbery and death of the pharmacy owner. Nor has he learned any lessons about the importance of love, loyalty, and friendship. In fact, he's far from becoming an adult. But his intent to review his film until he learns something about himself is a step in the right direction. Many young people do

The United States has the world's largest prison population: 2.3 million. There are more African Americans in its criminal justice system today than there were slaves in 1860.

things without considering the possible consequences. They lack the foresight that comes with maturity. If Steve can learn from his film where he went wrong and what he needs to do to prevent similar poor decisions from happening in the future, there is hope for him. Otherwise, he may very well turn into the "monster" the prosecuting attorney says he is and his father now believes he could possibly be.

Walter has published more words in more books and won more awards than any other African-American writer.

# Chapter 4
# WAIT! WAIT! THERE'S MORE!

Walter Dean Myers has written more than eighty-five books, totaling more pages than any other African-American author. The range includes science fiction, fantasy, history, fairy tales, biography, mystery, adventure, poetry, drama, and memoir as well as novels about African-American teenagers from the streets of Harlem. He's also won numerous awards. *Hoops* was named an American Library Association Award winner for Best Book for Young Adults. *Fallen Angels* won a Coretta Scott King Author Award and was one of four of his books to win a Margaret A. Edwards Award recognizing his "significant and lasting contribution to young adult literature." Not to be outdone, *Monster* in 1999 took the top spot in the first Michael L. Printz competition, which honors the year's "best book written for teens, based entirely on its literary merit." Most recently, Walter was named Ambassador of Literature for Young Adults by the Library of Congress. And that's only the tip of the iceberg.

With the publication of his early novel *Fast Sam, Cool Clyde, and Stuff* in 1975, Walter joined a class of authors that includes James Joyce, Mark Twain, J.D. Salinger, Kurt Vonnegut, Maya Angelou, and Stephen King. What these writers share is having some of their

"Books took me to a place within myself that I have been exploring ever since."
—Walter Dean Myers

books banned in different parts of the United States. *Hoops* made the list in 1981 followed by *Fallen Angels* in 1988. On the all-time list of writers with the highest number of banned books, Walter ranks seventh.

The reason most often cited for the bans is profane language.

Although Walter avoids using the most offensive of four-letter words, the language spoken by the characters in his novels is often coarse. There's no question about it. What the censors fail to appreciate, however, is that one reason why some of the greatest works of literature are so memorable is the very same realness of language that they object to in Walter's works. He doesn't just tell

Walter ranks No. 7 on the list of writers with the greatest number of books banned in different communities in the United States.

us about life in Harlem and Vietnam—any sociologist or historian could do that—he puts us on the streets, at the courthouse, in the jungle, wherever the action takes us.

As a child, Walter loved to read, but little of what he read was about people like him and communities like his. His writing, then, fills for young people today the void that existed in his own life. It also provides an alternative to the ways African-American people are so often presented in the white dominant culture. He doesn't shy away from the misfits, criminals, and losers but includes along with them a range of characters that readers, for close to half a century, have come to admire, respect, and love.

"I write to give hope to those kids who are like the ones I knew— poor, troubled, treated indifferently by society, sometimes bolstered by family and many times not."
—Walter Dean Myers

## WHY WALTER DEAN MYERS WRITES:

"I love writing. It is not something that I am doing just for a living; this is something that I love to do. I've been writing since I was nine. My writing was about the only thing I was praised for in school. I'm surprised to actually be able to make money doing this thing I love.

"I write to give hope to those kids who are like the ones I knew—poor, troubled, treated indifferently by society, sometimes bolstered by family and many times not.

"Ultimately what I want to do with my writing is make connections—to touch the lives of my characters and, through them, those of my readers."

# BOOKS BY
# WALTER DEAN MYERS

*Amistad: A Long Road to Freedom* (Dutton, 1998)

*At Her Majesty's Request: An African Princess in Victorian England* (Scholastic, 1999)

*Brown Angels: An Album of Picture and Verse* (HarperCollins, 1993)

*Fallen Angels* (Scholastic, 1988)

*The Glory Field* (Scholastic, 1994)

*Harlem: A Poem* (Scholastic, 1997)

*Hoops* (Laurel Leaf, 1983)

*It Ain't All for Nothin'* (HarperCollins, 2003)

*Malcolm X: A Fire Burning Brightly* (HarperCollins, 2000)

*Monster* (HarperCollins, 1999)

*Motown and Didi: A Love Story* (Laurel Leaf, 1987)

*The Mouse Rap* (HarperCollins, 1990)

*Now Is Your Time: The African-American Struggle for Freedom* (HarperCollins, 1991)

*145th Street: Short Stories* (Delacorte, 2000)

*One More River to Cross: An African-American Photograph Album* (Harcourt Brace, 1965)

*The Righteous Revenge of Artemis Bonner* (HarperCollins, 1992)

*Scorpions* (HarperCollins, 1988)

*Slam* (Scholastic, 1996)

*Somewhere in the Darkness* (Scholastic, 1992)

*Toussaint L'Ouverture: The Fight for Haiti's Freedom* (Simon & Schuster, 1996)

*The Young Landlords* (Puffin, 1992)

# GLOSSARY

**AK-47**—lightweight, automatic assault rifle. This weapon was heavily used by the Vietcong during the Vietnam War

**communism**—a theory or social system in which all property is owned in common, and all economic activity is determined by a centrally controlled government

**dog tag**—metal tag worn around the neck by people in the military. The tag states the wearer's name, social security number, blood type, and sometimes the person's religious affiliation

**gung ho**—enthusiastic, extremely loyal to a cause

**homeboy**—a term used to recognize a young or adult male from one's hometown, neighborhood, or close group of companions

**pacifist**—someone who is opposed to war or violence of any kind

**posse**—a group of friends who often gather socially; also called a "crew" or "homeboys"

**stiletto**—a short dagger with a thin blade

**Vietcong**—short for Vietnamese Communist. The Vietcong, largely supported with weapons and volunteer soldiers by the communist government of North Vietnam, was a guerrilla army fighting against the United States for control of South Vietnam during the Vietnam War

# CHRONOLOGY

**August 12, 1937:** Walter Milton Myers is born in Martinsburg, West Virginia.

**1940:** Walter is informally adopted by Herbert and Florence Dean after his mother dies in childbirth.

**1954:** Walter drops out of Stuyvesant High School and joins the United States Army on his seventeenth birthday.

**1959:** Walter marries Joyce Smith. He works in a post office.

**1961:** Joyce Myers gives birth to Karen Elaine. Walter plays basketball with the Jolly Brown Giants.

**1963:** Joyce has a second child, Michael Dean.

**1966:** Walter enrolls at City College under the GI Bill. He passes French but fails English.

**1968:** Walter becomes a pacifist after his twenty-one-year-old brother dies in Vietnam. *Where Does the Day Go?* wins first prize in a contest held by the Council on Interracial Books for Children. It becomes Walter's first published book. Joyce divorces Walter and takes Karen and Michael to live with her.

**1970:** Walter is hired as an acquisitions editor at Bobbs-Merrill and publishes the first prose book by Nikki Giovanni. Within one year, he is promoted to senior trade editor.

**1971:** With *The Dancers*, Walter changes his middle name from Milton to Dean to honor his adoptive parents.

**1974:** Walter marries Constance Brendel, and their son Christopher is born.

**1977:** The department in which Walter works at Bobbs-Merrill is closed, and Walter decides to become a full-time writer. He and Constance buy a house in Jersey City, New Jersey.

**1981:** Walter wins critical acclaim for *Hoops*. A film version stars Lou Gossett, Jr.

**1984:** Walter earns a bachelor's degree from the Empire State College program for adult learners and coaches Christopher's Little League baseball team.

**1986:** Walter's adoptive father Herbert dies of cancer, and Walter learns why his father never commented specifically on any of his books: he couldn't read.

**1988:** Walter wins a fellowship to the prestigious McDowell Colony in New Hampshire. *Fallen Angels* wins Walter his third Coretta Scott King Award, fifth American Library Association Best Book for Young Adults Award, and second Parents' Choice Award.

**1989:** The American Library Association adds *Hoops* to its list of books banned anywhere in the United States.

**1994:** Walter wins the first annual Virginia Hamilton Award and his sixth Coretta Scott King Award for *Malcolm X* as well as the Margaret A. Edwards Award for lifetime achievement in writing for young adults.

**1999:** Walter publishes *Monster*. His son Chris illustrates the text with photos, some of which are accentuated with his father's fingerprints. The novel wins a National Book Award nomination and another Coretta Scott King Award.

**2000:** Walter captures seventh place out of the top ten most censored authors during Banned Book Week in late September.

**2005:** According to the American Library Association, *Fallen Angels* is the number one banned book in the United States.

**2012:** The English Speaking Union of Great Britain names Walter an Ambassador of African-American Literature for Young Adults.

**2013:** Scholastic Press publishes a twenty-fifth anniversary edition of *Fallen Angels*.

# FURTHER INFORMATION

## Books

Are you interested in trying to write stories yourself? These two books offer guidance:

Levine, Gail Carson. *Writing Magic.* New York: Collins, 2006.

Messner, Kate. *Real Revision: Authors' Strategies to Share with Student Writers.* Portland, ME: Stenhouse, 2011.

## Websites

www.harpercollinschildrens.com

www.walterdeanmyers.net/biblio.html

# BIBLIOGRAPHY

## Books

Bishop, Rudine Sims. *Presenting Walter Dean Myers.*
  Boston: Twayne Press, 1991.

Myers, Walter Dean. *Bad Boy: A Memoir.* New York: Harper Tempest, 2001.

_____. *Fallen Angels.* New York: Scholastic Press, 1988.

_____. *Hoops.* New York: Ember, 1981.

_____. *Monster,* New York: Amistad, 1999.

Snodgrass, Mary Ellen. *Walter Dean Myers: A Literary Companion.*
  Jefferson, NC: McFarland & Co., 2006.

Zitlow, Connie S. *Teaching the Selected Works of Walter Dean Myers.*
  Portsmouth, NH: Heinemann, 2007.

## ONLINE SOURCES

www.authors4teens.com

www.harpercollinschildrens.com

www.walterdeanmyers.net

# INDEX

# ABOUT THE AUTHOR:

Richard Andersen teaches writing and literature at Springfield College in Massachusetts. A former Fulbright professor and James Thurber Writer-in-Residence, he has published twenty-six books, won his college's Excellence in Teaching Award, and was nominated for the Carnegie Foundation's United States Professor of the Year Award. Richard's first book for young people, *A Home Run for Bunny*, was published in 2013. Richard lives in Montague, Massachusetts, with his extraordinary wife Diane.